TENNYSON AND HIS CIRCLE

Lynne Truss

NPG

Published in Great Britain by National Portrait Gallery Publications,
National Portrait Gallery, St Martin's Place, London WC2H 0HE

ISBN 1 85514 257 0

A catalogue record for this book is available from the British Library

Series Project Editors: Celia Jones and Lucy Clark
Series Picture Researcher: Susie Foster
Series Designer: Karen Stafford
Printed by Clifford Press Ltd, Coventry

Front cover
Alfred Tennyson, 1st Baron Tennyson, 1809–92
William Henry Margetson, 1891 (detail)
Watercolour, 32.7 x 24.1cm
National Portrait Gallery (4343)
© Estate of William Henry Margetson

For a complete catalogue of current publications,
please write to the address above.

CONTENTS

❦

Introduction   *4*

Select Bibliography   *13*

Alfred Tennyson, 1st Baron Tennyson (1809–92)   *14*

Emily Tennyson (1813–96), Hallam Tennyson (1852–1928)
  AND Lionel Tennyson (1854–86)   *22*

Julia Margaret Cameron (1815–79)   *26*

George Frederic Watts (1817–1904)   *31*

The Much Photographed Household at Dimbola   *35*

Ellen Terry (1847–1928)   *40*

Henry Taylor (1800–86)   *48*

Edward Lear (1812–88)   *50*

'Pattledom': The Pattle Family   *52*

Charles Lutwidge Dodgson (Lewis Carroll) (1832–98)   *56*

'Hiawatha's Photographing', by Lewis Carroll   *62*

List of Illustrations   *64*

ALFRED TENNYSON, 1ST BARON TENNYSON, George Frederic Watts, *c.*1863–4

INTRODUCTION

Writing to his good friend Julia Margaret Cameron in the 1860s, G. F. Watts told her, 'Do justice to the noble and beautiful head. It is the finest you will ever have before your lens.' The head in question was the poet Alfred Tennyson's; the advice kindly but superfluous. If there was one thing Mrs Cameron prided herself on, it was doing justice to the big intellectual heads of Victorian England. 'Big eyes, big eyes!' she would boom at her illustrious sitters – Tennyson, Browning, Carlyle – as they held their solemn poses for a painful five-minute exposure, without the aid of a neck-brace. At her makeshift studio at Dimbola, her house at Freshwater Bay on the Isle of Wight, she would position her sitters in a flattering pool of light that showed their massive brows and fabulous beards to the utmost advantage. She would try to make them look as if they had been carved in stone. 'She considers it a great privilege to be done by her,' remarked the poet William Allingham in his diary, sounding unconvinced. But if she did so, she had every right.

Had Mrs Cameron not been such a tireless bride of art, the Tennyson circle would of course still be accessible to us today in portraits, but the period would appear very differently – more functional, flatter, more remote. The 1860s, when many of the pictures in this book were produced, was a decade of vitality and progress in England, yet just at the point when the idea of celebrity was taking hold, conventional portraiture ran into a crisis. The advent of mass photography at a stroke deprived the portrait artist of his former, practical *raison d'être* – to record for unborn generations the faces of the great (or rich, or royal). In 1851 the chemical accident of gun cotton dissolved in ether had created the famous 'wet collodion' process for coating a photographic plate, and from then on portraiture was arguably achieved by the fairly simple means of a sitter exposing himself directly to a camera plate.

The dramatic impact on the world of art is easily seen. As David Piper points out in his book *The English Face*, Royal Academy exhibition statistics trace the dramatic decline of the portrait genre. In 1830 over half the Royal Academy pictures were portraits, whereas by 1870 the proportion had dropped to one-fifth. Meanwhile, unsurprisingly, the painting of miniatures had all but ceased. Against this background, it is not surprising that a serious artist such as Watts would make elevated claims for his own project – a 'Hall of Fame' series of portraits to be donated to the nation – and to take the motto 'The Utmost for the Highest'. Mrs Cameron, meanwhile, insisted that photography itself could be dedicated to art in the same pious way, so that a photograph of a great man could be described as 'almost the embodiment of prayer'.

Public interest in famous faces did not decline; quite the reverse. Through photography, it burgeoned. Real faces could now be studied universally, and the high Victorian period saw an explosion of interest in physiognomy, phrenology and any other science by which it was thought a person's moral nature could be judged by externals. 'Nature never writes a bad hand,' Charles Dickens wrote in 1856 in his weekly paper *Household Words*. 'Her writing, as it may be read in the human countenance, is invariably legible, if we come at all trained to the reading of it.' To modern ears this sounds like superstition, prejudice, or even insanity, but it is hard to argue with Dickens in dogmatic mode. And on that occasion he had just observed the poisoner William Palmer in the dock, so spoke from incontrovertible first hand. 'The physiognomy and conformation of the Poisoner,' he recorded, 'were exactly in accordance with his deeds; and every guilty consciousness he had gone on storing in his mind, had set its mark upon him.'

Faces fell neatly into types and categories; it sometimes seems that a person was only as good as the span of inches between his eyebrow and his earlobe. When W. P. Frith's famous crowd picture *Derby Day* was first exhibited at the Royal Academy in 1858, its various tableaux were studied avidly by visitors intent on spotting the various moral types depicted – including a man in a topper who corresponded to the 'Thurtell type'. We look at him now and see a quite handsome face, possibly a bit sly – but to Victorian eyes, his thick eyebrows, narrow forehead and small eyes marked him out as the model of the cold-blooded murderer John Thurtell (1794–1824). It was understood that anyone with such features was preordained to be villainous by nature, just as a girl's bulging forehead would signify her virtue.

One begins to get the impression that the adage 'It takes all sorts to make a world' was not heard much in Victorian artistic circles. But at least it explains why good girls in Dickens illustrations always look as if their heads are about to explode.

Big foreheads were the only acceptable thing, because phrenologists argued that perceptive and moral organs resided in the brow and dome. The Pre-Raphaelite Holman Hunt painted a squat-browed Semitic Christ, and was berated for it. (He was even criticised in some quarters for the expressions he gave to his sheep.) Meanwhile, Alfred Tennyson may not strike us now as particularly handsome, but his high brow was displayed to great effect in his many portraits, while the massive bags under his eyes were proof enough (to the phrenologically initiated) not that he had smoked too much and slept too little, but that he had a great natural facility for Language (the Organ of Language was under the eye).

Lips, noses, jaws – all had their meanings to those equipped with the right glossary. A book by Eden Warwick called *Notes on Noses* (1852) declared, without any shade of a double-meaning, 'There is more in a nose than most owners of that appendage are generally aware.' Meanwhile that arch-rationalist Thomas Carlyle based his objection to the Elgin Marbles on the fact that there was not a single 'clever' face among those portrayed, as the jaws were not sufficiently prominent. 'Depend upon it,' he told Watts, during a portrait sitting, 'neither God nor man can get on without a jaw.'

In the same surreal conversation (recorded in *Annals of a Painter's Life* by Watts's devoted widow Mary) Carlyle goes on to

Woolner at Farringford, 1857: 'Mrs Tennyson, "You know, Mr Woolner, I'm the most unmeddlesome of women, but – when (I am only asking) when do you begin modelling his halo"', Max Beerbohm, 1917

7

JULIA MARGARET CAMERON, attributed to Lord Somers, n.d.

declare the long upper lip a sign of intellect, at which point Watts argues back. Look at the short lips of Napoleon, Byron and Goethe, he says. Finally, they alight on the only feature left – the eye. All right then, says Watts, does the brown or grey eye denote the man of action? Carlyle says brown, but Watts demurs again, quoting a first-hand report of Napoleon's 'steel-cold' eyes. Napoleon, it seems, was never left out of such discussions for long. However, Carlyle finally caps the pigment debate by sending Watts an account of 'Mahomet', whose eyes were 'large, black and full of fire'. Which seems to have put an end to it.

Nobody had a picture of Mahomet at home, of course. It was not possible to check. But with the boom of photography in the mid-century, we enter the era of the *carte-de-visite*, when portraiture finally became everyday. *Cartes-de-visite* (such as the picture of Edward Lear on page 51) were all the rage in the 1860s – an early precursor of the mania for cigarette cards. If you had a *carte-de-visite* of Queen Victoria it did not mean she had been to your house; it just meant you had liked her picture enough to buy it. People could collect mass-produced likenesses of the royal family, statesmen and poets, stick them in albums and study them for edification.

Tennyson abhorred this development (he was not progressive in many things); while enjoying the benefits of celebrity, he decried the drawbacks. He was a private man, and he disliked the idea that he owed anything to the people who bought his books. In particular he told his Isle of Wight neighbour Mrs Cameron that as a result of her 'confounded' photographs, innkeepers on the mainland recognised his face and charged him double. The story goes that once, at Farringford (his home at Freshwater), he looked up to see a strange woman's face pressed against the window; she was calling to friends 'You can see him quite well from here.' Shakespeare, he often observed, was lucky to live in an age in which the facts of his life were of no interest to the public.

But how lucky for Tennyson, in retrospect, that the photographers and artists who admired and surrounded him had such high-minded ideals. What Watts wanted to achieve in portraiture was a great deal more than a surface likeness; in rather mystical language, he said that what he tried for was 'the half-conscious insistence on the nobilities of the subject'. Tennyson may have disliked being a literary lion, but he ultimately benefited from

The Late Lord Tennyson: Mr G. F. Watts, RA, painting the Poet Laureate's Portrait in the Study at Farringford, Reginald Cleaver, 1892

his enthusiastic lionisers, to whom the flat, functional art of the *carte-de-visite* was abomination. Just as Watts had counselled her, Mrs Cameron saw it as her privilege and duty to glorify a great, important head like Tennyson's. She was apt to introduce her friends as 'the greatest living poet' and the 'greatest living Indian legislator'. Superlatives were her meat and drink. Her pictures were enormous, and prints were personally signed. Photography, which she took up as a hobby at the end of 1863, was a perfect extension of her talent for feeding other people's egos. It required energy, persuasiveness and patience. And although she did not have very much of the third, she had impressive amounts of the other two.

Meanwhile Watts's portraiture was a massive achievement. After his death in 1904, his widow Mary catalogued the hundreds of portraits he had painted in a career spanning the whole length of Queen Victoria's reign. The result, now at the Victoria and Albert Museum, was a book of 175 pages, with at least three images on each. In neat tabular form, Mrs Watts gives the title, the size and the date of each portrait, together with notes on its owner, its exhibitions and a short account of the sittings. Wherever possible, she also records how well the 'nobilities' of the picture's subject were attained. One entry describes Watts's third portrait of Sir Frederic Leighton PRA, painted in 1890, six years before his death:

> *Soon after Lord Leighton's death, Professor Herkomer, speaking to Mr Watts, recalled the dignified bearing of their* [the Royal Academy's] *president as they sat around him in the council room, and used the words 'He had the aspect of a greek god as he sat amongst us.' And this, surely, his painter has portrayed.*

One sitter wrote to Watts, 'If on my approaching leave-taking of this life I am not at once forgotten, it will be due to the survival not of anything which I have left, but to the work of your hand.' Testimonials of this sort were not uncommon. Both Watts and Mrs Cameron believed in bestowing immortality, and if part of this book deals with the pretty maids, sisters,

GEORGE FREDERIC WATTS (with a cast for his sculpture *Physical Energy*), Henry Herschel Hay Cameron, n.d.

children and butcher's lads Mrs Cameron's work recorded, it shows above all the power of the successful portrait to reach across time and obscure other faces from view.

The result of this, strangely, is that there are more decent pictures of an obscure woman known simply as 'Mrs Donkin's cook' than there are of George Eliot – and the reason is bound up with the period's enslavement to beauty. The camera could not lie enough. To people who believed a lovely soul made a lovely face (let us call it the cosmetic fallacy), the phenomenon of an unattractive genius, such as George Eliot, presented problems. Eliot's features did not fit the bill, aesthetically or physiognomically. Both Watts and Mrs Cameron came comically unstuck in the presence of people whose features flouted the rules.

For example, when Watts requested the chance to paint Benjamin Jowett, the round-faced Master of Balliol, he 'found his subject the most difficult he ever attempted'. Mary Watts explains in the V&A's catalogue that her husband was baffled by Jowett's inadequate face: 'The Master he so reverenced had not the features to explain his great eminence.' Similarly, Watts would have painted George Eliot for the Hall of Fame, but knew 'that the features belonged to a type he would have found most difficult; and afraid of not doing the great mind justice, he did not venture to make the attempt'. Under the same pressure to photograph an ugly woman, Mrs Cameron coined an instant universal rule: 'No woman should be photographed between the ages of 18 and 80.' And with a single bound (and a sigh of relief), she was free.

SELECT BIBLIOGRAPHY

Michael Bakewell, *Lewis Carroll: A Biography*, Heinemann, London, 1996.

Wilfrid Blunt, *England's Michelangelo: A Biography of George Frederic Watts*, Hamish Hamilton, London, 1975.

Morton N. Cohen, *Lewis Carroll: A Biography*, Macmillan, London, 1995.

Mary Cowling, *The Artist as Anthropologist: The Representation of Type and Character in Victorian Art*, Cambridge University Press, 1989.

Colin Ford, *The Cameron Collection: An Album of Photographs by Julia Margaret Cameron Presented to Sir John Herschel*, Van Nostrand Reinhold/National Portrait Gallery, London, 1975.

Helmut Gernsheim, *Lewis Carroll, Photographer*, Dover Books, New York, 1969.

Helmut Gernsheim, *Julia Margaret Cameron*, Gordon Fraser, London, 1975.

Brian Hill, *Julia Margaret Cameron: A Victorian Family Portrait*, Peter Owen, London, 1973.

Amanda Hopkinson, *Julia Margaret Cameron*, Virago, London, 1986.

Derek Hudson, *Lewis Carroll*, Constable, London, 1954.

Peter Levi, *Edward Lear*, Macmillan, London, 1995.

Roger Manvell, *Ellen Terry*, Heinemann, London, 1968.

Robert Bernard Martin, *Tennyson: The Unquiet Heart*, Faber and Faber, London, 1980.

Leonée Ormond, *Tennyson and Thomas Woolner*, The Tennyson Society, Lincoln, 1981.

Norman Page (ed.), *Tennyson: Interviews and Recollections*, Macmillan, London, 1983.

David Piper, *The English Face*, Thames and Hudson, 1957; National Portrait Gallery, 1978, 1992.

Ann Thwaite, *Emily Tennyson: The Poet's Wife*, Faber and Faber, London, 1996.

Mike Weaver, *Julia Margaret Cameron, 1815–1879*, The Herbert Press, London, 1984.

Mike Weaver, *British Photography in the Nineteenth Century: The Fine Art Tradition*, Cambridge University Press, 1989.

Sylvia Wolf, *Julia Margaret Cameron's Women*, The Art Institute of Chicago/Yale University Press, New Haven and London, 1998.

ALFRED TENNYSON, 1ST BARON TENNYSON
(1809–92)

❧

His great friend James Spedding once said of Alfred Tennyson that he was a man 'always discontented with the present till it has become the past, and then he yearns for it, and worships it, and not only worships it but is discontented because it is past.'

Of all the written descriptions of Tennyson, few have helped us read his portraits as well as this. In photographs and busts it is much harder to discover the selfish, virile and astonishing man who could pronounce ill-temperedly 'Legs of mutton should be cut in wedges!' when introduced to an admirer. But Tennyson as a dismayed prophet seeing his own life through a mirror, like the Lady of Shalott – yearning, discontented – this man you can see in the portraits, from those of his adolescence to those of his great old age. True, short-sightedness could equally well account for the faraway look in his eyes (he once ran away from a flock of sheep, thinking they were autograph-hunters). He also, after 1852, wore false teeth that did not fit, so a smile was out of the question. But if his poetry did not already reveal his preoccupation with the past, and with grief, his demeanour in his portraits infallibly betrays a fiercely private man focused on the middle distance, baffled by the enigma of time.

He had ample reason for his discontent. Just being a Tennyson was no joke. He was born in 1809, at Somersby, Lincolnshire, into an uncouth, eccentric and enormous family, and the fact that his brother Septimus once introduced himself with the words 'I am Septimus, most morbid of all the Tennysons' unfortunately says it all. Somersby Rectory was hardly the loving nursery of genius. Tennyson's father, the Reverend George Clayton Tennyson, was a depressed, disappointed and possibly violent man; according to legend, he was once actually unable to remember his own name until someone called 'Good evening, Dr Tennyson'. Dr Tennyson was an elder son with expectations, but was disinherited by his father ('The Old Man of the Wolds') on account of unfilial outbursts. Meanwhile Alfred's beautiful, well-born invalid mother was pulled around in a carriage by a St Bernard, a choice that makes her sound refreshingly larky in all this saturnine gloom.

Unsurprisingly, the twelve Tennyson children did not escape unscathed from such an upbringing; they suffered variously from epilepsy, insanity, heightened poetic sensibility, bad eyesight, accidents with coal-scuttles, and (later) abject opium addiction. Alfred learned as a boy to put himself in an abstracted, trance-like state by saying his own name over and over – what modern psychologists would call a survival mechanism. Though always tiresomely haunted by the 'black blood of the Tennysons', the poet clearly deserves the utmost congratulation for evading his genetic destiny. As Robert Bernard Martin writes in his biography, 'It has been customary to marvel over Tennyson's morbidity and gloom, but it would be more to the point to wonder at the strength of character that kept his mind from total disintegration.'

What Tennyson took from this childhood, it seems, was mainly fear: fear of madness, and fear of poverty. He also learned to guard his privacy – which meant that although he rose to Poet Laureate (in 1850), he was never happy to be a public figure. He loved the praise, attention and money that came with fame, but disliked the price of celebrity. Why should the lives of poets be raked over by strangers (or 'ripped open like pigs')? Retirement was therefore much more in Tennyson's nature; hence his decision to live on the furthest corner of the Isle of Wight, and to run away from 'cockneys'. Solitude and dangerous self-absorption form the staple of many of his most famous poems, too.

Among his earliest portraits, from his short career at Cambridge, are three pencil sketches attributed to his friend Spedding, one of which is reproduced here. In all three pictures he holds an object unnaturally close to his nose (here, a book), and his posture cries aloud

ALFRED TENNYSON, 1ST BARON TENNYSON, attributed to James Spedding, *c.*1831

15

for the urgent invention of either reading-spectacles or the light-bulb. These amateur sketches do not tell us very much, perhaps, until we compare them with Spedding's pencil sketch of Tennyson's accomplished young Cambridge friend Arthur Henry Hallam (1811–33). Hallam likewise holds a book, but clearly is not reading it. Hallam is erect, graceful, head bent slightly; he has even combed his hair. Tennyson is hunched almost double over his reading, and if you look at the picture for a few seconds, the book seems to travel closer to his nose. Later in life, Tennyson's wife Emily dismissed the arrival of a set of pictures of Alfred – 'these semblances of biography which are no biography,' she called them. It seems odd that she could not see their value.

Tennyson's Cambridge days gave him a coterie of admiring, wealthy friends – notable among them Hallam, whose early death so famously inspired Tennyson's monumental *In Memoriam A.H.H.* (1850). Tennyson was already a published poet by the time he matriculated to Trinity College in 1828, and Cambridge further encouraged his poetry. Taking a degree was optional at this time. His 'Timbuctoo' was awarded the Chancellor's Medal for English verse in June 1829. The publication of Tennyson's first solo collection, *Poems Chiefly Lyrical*, came in 1830, when he was twenty-one. He left Cambridge without a degree the following year, saying that the university had 'taught him nothing, feeding not the heart'. But he had made friends with clever men who enjoyed his 'humours and grumpiness', who would support him in various ways all his life, and for whose delight he would evidently perform hilarious impressions of the sun breaking through cloud, or of His Majesty George IV.

If Tennyson's youth had been ill-starred, his twenties and thirties were worse. In fact, they were terrible. He was always touchy about criticism, and a bad review of his *Poems* (1833) – which included such pieces as 'The Lady of Shalott' and 'A Dream of Fair Women' – wounded him so badly that he was sent off course for nearly ten years. In particular, he shelved his ideas for a big Arthurian poem, which as a consequence did not begin to take shape until 1859, when his first edition of *Idylls of the King* was published (the definitive version appeared in 1872). If the review had wounded him, the death of Hallam in Vienna in September 1833 was devastating. Hallam was not only his best friend and mentor, but the fiancé of Tennyson's

ALFRED TENNYSON, 1ST BARON TENNYSON, Samuel Laurence, c.1840

sister Emily. Suddenly, Tennyson saw a future with nothing in it. For the next seventeen years he led a rootless existence, smoking to excess, drinking unwisely, indulging his grief in great lyric poems such as 'Tears, Idle Tears', 'Ulysses' and 'Morte d'Arthur', and remembering to keep body and soul together mainly by turning up at friends' houses ('coming unwashed and staying unbidden') in expectation of a meal and a bed.

From 1840 we have both a description and a portrait. Interestingly, aside from their overall colour (brown) they could not be less alike. This is how Thomas Carlyle described him, unkempt and wreathed in smoke:

A fine large-featured, dim-eyed, bronze-coloured, shaggy-headed man is Alfred; dusty, smoky, free-and-easy: who swims, outwardly and inwardly,

with great composure in an inarticulate element as of tranquil chaos and
tobacco smoke; great now and then when he does emerge: a most restful,
brotherly, solidhearted man.

Send schoolchildren around the National Portrait Gallery to locate this
man's likeness, and it is unlikely they would discover it in Samuel Laurence's
romantic canvas. It is a beautiful portrait – although Tennyson himself called
the picture 'blubber-lipt' – but if you did not know the sitter's occupa-
tion, you might easily guess man of action, or radical parliamentarian. Edward
FitzGerald (translator of the *Rubáiyát of Omar Khayyám*) persuaded Tennyson
to sit for Laurence, who afterwards said that Tennyson was the strongest-
minded man he had ever met. Whether that opinion was reflected adversely
in the original canvas we shall never know, because after Tennyson's death,
Edward Burne-Jones was requested to repaint the picture, and tame it. Perhaps the offence in the picture was that it supported the general (false)
assumption about Tennyson: that he was an opium addict. The family were
always keen to stamp out this particular slander.

Yet escape into an opium daze might have been quite a good idea at this
time for Tennyson. Financial disasters, hydropathic cures, emotional break-
down and a broken engagement were the background to his 1840s. His
stature as a poet was growing, however. His two-volume *Poems* of 1842
was, thankfully, well reviewed, but he was still poor, relying on a Civil List
pension and gifts from friends, rather than taking paid work. Later in
life Tennyson refused to give up the Civil List pension (intended for
relief from financial misery), even when he was earning £10,000 a year.
He resented the assumption he was rich, and always claimed to be poor.
There was no arguing with him, apparently, on this point. When made a
peer in 1884, he even managed to evade paying the statutory expenses.

Mercifully, the flat-line graph of Tennyson's fortunes finally took an
upturn on the exact pivot of the century. It was like the sun breaking through
cloud. On completion of his hydropathic cures, he decided to disbelieve (at
last) in the black blood of the Tennysons; meanwhile his poem *The Princess*
(1847) was selling well. He pounced on the opportunity (at last) to
marry Emily Sellwood, the saintly thirty-seven-year-old to whom he
had been engaged, on and off, for thirteen years, and it was a decision

he would never regret. 'The peace of God came
into my life before the altar when I wed-
ded her,' he declared. With Emily, his life
acquired stability, affection and, above all,
organisation. On holiday in the Lake District
shortly after their marriage, she sent him out
for long walks, and when she found that he walked
straight past their house on his return, she had the
gate-posts painted white to attract his attention. She
was uncritical and practical: the sort of person he needed.

So 1850 was Tennyson's breakthrough year. Within a couple of months,
William Wordsworth died (freeing the post of Poet Laureate), and *In Memoriam* was published to huge acclaim. *In Memoriam* is an immense poem,
which had been written over a period of seventeen years, acquiring ever
more depth and refinement. In it Tennyson explores the power of artistic intuition to make sense of life and death. It is an internal piece, as
Tennyson's best work always is. Although he sometimes tried his hand
at drama, Tennyson had no interest in (or understanding for) another
person's point of view. When his poetry is true to himself, it rings clear like
a bell; when he is faking compassion, it clunks.

Would Tennyson be the next Poet Laureate? He said afterwards that he
dithered over whether to accept (the post brought only £100), but of course
he did, and the next ten years were the best of his life. There was travel and
happiness, and more financial success. Although a first child was stillborn,
Emily gave birth to Hallam (1852) and Lionel (1854). Friendships accrued
with William Allingham, Edward Lear, the Camerons, Watts, and more
cautiously with Robert Browning, whose poetry Tennyson thought lacking
in music. The family moved from Twickenham to Farringford in 1853, which
they took on a lease when both Alfred and Emily fell in love with the view
of cliffs and sea. They invited friends to stay, but since Tennyson's principal means of entertaining them was to read his own poetry for two or
three hours at a stretch, some of them did not come back. Tennyson's
controversial monodrama *Maud* (1855) sold so well that he bought Farringford outright, and began to improve it. From being a virtual down-and-out
ten years before, he was now an Eminent Victorian.

ALFRED TENNYSON, 1ST BARON TENNYSON, Julia Margaret Cameron, 1869

Portraits abound from this period onwards, but Mrs Cameron's 1869 'Dirty Monk' picture is the one that perhaps encompasses most successfully iconography and the real man, ascetic and pauper, plus grandeur and bathos. Tennyson's pose, beard and hairline are grand, Italianate, compelling; yet the neck is dirty, the hand and fingernails huge and beefy. Even as a great photograph, it has one perfect flaw: the long drip suspended forever in front of Tennyson reminds us that, unbelievably, this image is really an arrangement of chemicals persuaded to cling to a photographic plate.

By the time the 'Dirty Monk' was taken, Tennyson was the foremost literary lion in England. His collection of 1864, *Enoch Arden*, sold better than any previous volume, and according to his entry in the *Dictionary of National Biography* was translated into Danish, German, Latin, Dutch, Italian, French, Hungarian and Bohemian. He was secure in the esteem of his peers and even of the queen. The wife of the headmaster of Marlborough College put aside the cup he drank from, and treasured it. At home, visitors would listen to a reading of his 'Guinevere' and say that the poem would 'only die with the language in which it was written'. At which the ever-faithful Emily would chorus her agreement.

In 1868 the Tennysons started to build another home, at Aldworth in Surrey – the popularity of Freshwater Bay with unwanted visitors in summer made Tennyson seek a second home, and at Aldworth he could build a more secluded (and more baronial) Gothic hideaway. Fears that his poetic powers were waning, as he reached his sixtieth year, were refuted with the 1872 publication of a heavily revised and augmented *Idylls of the King*. It is not his most accomplished work, but it was decidedly popular – and its romantic Arthurian tableaux were to prove inspirational for Mrs Cameron. Tennyson was offered a baronetcy, but declined. What he wanted (and finally got) was a peerage.

His last twenty years were characterised by comfort, mainly in the company of sycophants who forgave his bearish eccentricity, his addiction to port and tobacco, and his social awkwardness. His reputation for bad manners reached new heights; asked by a hostess what he thought of a particular dish cooked in his honour, he said it tasted 'like an old boot'. 'Do you know anything about *Lowell*?' he asked Emily, entering for dinner and peering about. 'Why, my dear, this *is* Mr Lowell,' said Emily. A man called Oscar Browning introduced himself, 'I'm Browning.' Tennyson looked at him closely and said 'No, you're not.'

What drove Tennyson at this time of life to write for the theatre is a mystery, but suddenly out they came: big verse plays on historical themes, *Queen Mary* (1875) and *Becket* (1884). 'Tennyson is a great poet,' Henry Irving said, 'but he cannot write plays. What a pity he tries, they are the greatest rubbish!' But he persisted with a run of dramas, and in old age was finally seen to be beyond criticism, which was nice. Old friends died, Emily's strength began to fail, his son Hallam became his helpmeet in her place, and Tennyson decided to nominate Hallam as his official biographer. In 1886 Lionel Tennyson died at sea, returning from India – a desperately unhappy event for the family that reopened all Tennyson's old grief at the death of Arthur Hallam, fifty years before.

By the time Tennyson himself died, at Aldworth, an official, respectable version of his life was well prepared. Hallam had been briefed, the repainting of the Samuel Laurence portrait was in hand, and Tennyson's great last poem 'Crossing the Bar' had been composed in 1889. 'The process of making Tennyson's memory respectable,' writes Robert Bernard Martin, 'was so successful that it took another half-century before the world began to suspect that behind the bland features of the Watts portraits . . . was the complicated mind and awkward personality of one of England's greatest poets.'

EMILY TENNYSON (1813–96), HALLAM TENNYSON (1852–1928) AND LIONEL TENNYSON (1854–86)

❦

At the age of eleven, Emily Tennyson (née Sellwood) won the only prize of her life. It was for 'application', and no one who knows about the Tennysons' home life will be the least surprised. 'Application' might have been her middle name. Wife to the poet from 1850 to his death in 1892, Emily Tennyson was a clever, hard-working and energetically conventional woman, who applied herself continually in the shadows of her husband's fame.

It is no coincidence that when Tennyson's career finally lifted off in 1850, Emily was at his side, for she was as much his manager as his wife. Tennyson famously said he would 'as soon kill a pig as write a letter'; Emily therefore wrote most of the letters on his behalf, meanwhile also keeping accounts, running the household, and protecting Tennyson from bad reviews. Few authors allow another person to correct publishers' proofs, but Emily corrected Tennyson's. She even supplied titles for the volumes, and urged Alfred's friends to dream up subjects for him. It is hard to believe that the reputation of this delicate but intellectually lively woman – at least, until Ann Thwaite's biography was published in 1996 – was mainly for saintly invalidism.

W. Jeffrey's *carte-de-visite* of Emily Tennyson from the 1860s initially supports the invalid story. It also looks a formal and rather dull portrait of a woman in lace cap, hands folded, big frock, deep-set eyes. But there is something beautiful and secret in the sitter's expression that brings one back to it again and again. Carlyle said that the first glance of Emily was 'the least favourable' – and the same is true of this portrait. Carlyle continued, 'A freckly, round-faced woman, rather tallish and without shape, a slight lisp too . . . but she lights up bright glittering blue eyes when you speak to her.'

This picture was taken at Emily's happiest time, when her darling sons ('managed with kisses') were pretty, long-haired boys in big white collars and belted smocks, Tennyson's fortunes and reputation were increasing, and Farringford was a magnet for friends. Edward Lear, who was deeply fond of Emily, reported that 'the affection of the boys to her was beyond

EMILY TENNYSON, W. Jeffrey, 1860s

all idea', and in her published diaries she writes of excursions and holidays, and repeats the phrase, 'The boys were wild with delight'. As the linchpin of this improbably sunny household, the poet himself once ironed an alphabet on to cloth for the children; an image that once pictured never thereafter lapses from the mind.

Emily might never have had this domestic happiness, of course. She waited thirteen years for Tennyson to make up his mind to marry her, during which time he once broke off the engagement altogether. Complicating matters was another marriage between the two families: Alfred's brother Charles had wed Emily's sister Louisa in 1836, and the marriage had not been happy. Charles turned to opium addiction and Louisa became a religious maniac. This calamitous match cannot have encouraged either family to think of repeating the experiment. So Emily was left marooned, waiting in a Lincolnshire market town with her widowed father, reading German, immersing herself in family matters, and honing her talent for feminine selflessness.

Critics have suggested that Emily's uncritical support of Tennyson undermined him as a poet. If only she had not regarded him as a living saint, they say, he would have striven more for original forms; he would not have become complacent. Such criticism is unrealistic and unfair, since it is quite clear that an atmosphere of praise and attention was the only one Tennyson could tolerate, certainly the only one in which his genius could flourish. The idea that Tennyson would marry a critical woman is frankly hilarious. He met and admired George Eliot, luckily unaware she had written an anonymous attack on his morbidity in the *Westminster Review*. Once the two writers had became fond of one another, Tennyson praised her as far as his nature would allow; she was 'a humble woman', he said, despite 'a dogmatic manner of assertion that has come upon her latterly in her writings'.

The Tennyson boys each took after a parent. Hallam, the elder, was closer in nature to his mother. In photographs he appears shy, serious, pliable. When Emily's health failed in later life (when all the lying-down started), Hallam seems to have stepped into the breach and 'slaved' for them both. He succeeded to the title, and wrote the official biography. Once, on the eve of Hallam's birthday, Emily wrote a note to Alfred, in which she mapped out a poem Alfred could write for his son. It included the line,

'No idler hast thou been within our walls'. 'Ally mine,' she wrote, 'I want you to write something of this sort to our Hallam on his birthday. Begin it to day I beg of thee.' But there is no evidence he did.

Lionel was a very different personality. When the two boys are pictured together, it is hard to imagine Hallam is two years older than his brother. Hallam has a pleasant baby face; Lionel is precocious, a heart-breaker. At school, as an adult, and in his early death, Lionel caused

LIONEL TENNYSON, Julia Margaret Cameron, 1864

much grief and worry to the poet and his wife – a scandal at Eton, a flirtatious and forceful nature, and (probably) an adulterous marriage. Lionel's grandson Hallam Tennyson, in his autobiography *The Haunted Mind* (1984), describes Mrs Cameron's pictures of Lionel: 'The large, rather sullen mouth and the heavy-lidded eyes with their hint of egotism and sensuality make it probable that he had inherited far more of the "black bloodedness" of the Tennysons than his sweet natured brother.'

It is this latent danger in Lionel that makes him so attractive as a child, of course. Here, at ten years old, he is posing coquettishly as Cupid with a bow: Charles Lutwidge Dodgson ('Lewis Carroll') described him as 'the loveliest child, boy or girl, I ever saw' – a huge tribute from Dodgson, who generally detested boys. When Dodgson met the eight-year-old Lionel in 1862, he asked the child for some verses, and records in his diary that Lionel laid down two provisos, one of them rather startling. 'First, I was to play a game of chess with him . . . Second, he was to be allowed to give me one blow on the head with a mallet (this he at last consented to give up).'

JULIA MARGARET CAMERON (1815–79)

The only sad thing about Julia Margaret Cameron was that she was by far the least beautiful person she knew. Born into the glamorous Pattle family in Calcutta, she was nicknamed 'Talent', which sounds all right until you know two of her sisters were 'Beauty' and 'Dash'. Sensibly, she had no illusions about her own attractiveness, much as she revered beauty and pursued it. When Mr Peacock, an Isle of Wight visitor, one day remarked to her that plain people ought to be 'quietly eliminated', Mrs Cameron replied tartly, 'Then what would become of you and me, *Mr Pocock*?'

What is so shocking to fans of her photography, however, is that portraits of her do so little to capture the wild enthusiasm, the bossiness, the pure bustle for which she was famous. 'Mrs Cameron is making endless Madonnas and May Queens and Foolish Virgins and Wise Virgins,' Emily Tennyson marvelled to Edward Lear in 1865, 'It really is wonderful how she puts her spirit into people.' How odd, then, that she could not convey this infectious spirit when her own pictures were taken. From her surviving portraits, she looks exhausted. The best you would guess of her character is that – in her own words – she had 'fagged herself to the utmost'.

Mrs Cameron did not begin photographing until the end of 1863, when her daughter Julia gave her a camera as a present. She was then forty-eight years old, wife of a retired Indian jurist, and already living at Freshwater on the Isle of Wight, in a house just a few hundred yards from Tennyson's Farringford. She immediately started photographing family, friends, maids, children. Photography appealed to all her traits – she was tireless, curious, ambitious, pietistic and, above all, liked to be usefully employed while other people sat still.

'I longed to arrest all the beauty that came before me,' she wrote in 1874 in her unfinished autobiography *Annals of My Glass House*, and it was a fine impulse, even if 'That's funny, I feel as though I've been arrested' is how the sitters would have described the experience afterwards. 'Longfellow, you have to do whatever she tells you,' Tennyson earnestly advised his fellow poet, in 1868, 'I'll come back soon and see what is left of you.' That Mrs Cameron was not above bullying celebrities to appear in her photographs was clearly a source of affectionate amusement at the time, but

JULIA MARGARET CAMERON, Henry Herschel Hay Cameron, 1870

on the other hand, thank goodness she had such a forceful personality. Posterity has rather a lot to thank it for.

Luckily for us, Mrs Cameron's family background – among those beautiful and dashing Pattles – equipped her with plenty of nerve, as well as a celebrity fixation. The Pattles were great *salonniers*, and great flatterers, and Julia Margaret Cameron's sister Sara Prinsep presided at Little

THOMAS CARLYLE, Julia Margaret Cameron, 1867

Holland House over a very respectable *salon* indeed – frequented by Tennyson, the Rossettis, Carlyle, even Dickens. G. F. Watts made a permanent home there, and was accorded the reverential title 'Il Signor'. Hyperbolic levels of praise and hospitality were the key to the Pattles' social success, to which Mrs Cameron added a fearful enthusiasm for bestowing unwanted gifts.

People did sometimes complain of being 'Pattled', and it sounds quite dreadful. 'They were so sweet with each other, and so sweet to me, and overcame me so, with every kind of loving-kindness, that I was really upset, and fairly cried in Mrs Prinsep's face,' records a Mrs Twistleton, visiting from Boston. The poor woman had clearly been almost Pattled to death. Her experience is a useful yardstick, however. If the sisters would put on a show like that for a mere Mrs Twistleton of Boston, think what they would have done for the Poet Laureate.

As a photographer, Mrs Cameron had a single aim – to record faithfully 'the greatness of the inner as well as the features of the outer man'. She specialised in intellectuals, and concentrated on the seat of intellect, the head. Never interested in clothes or locality (and scornful of depth of field) she would wrap her subjects in bits of blanket or old cloaks, focus her lens until she found 'something beautiful' and then expose the picture. It irritated her when people said her pictures were out of focus – 'What *is* focus – and who has the right to say what focus is legitimate focus?' she asked.

It also annoyed her that a photograph by Henry Peach Robinson – called *Brenda* – was judged superior to her own luminous offerings the first time she exhibited, in 1864. *Brenda* sounds every bit as bathetic as the name implies. No wonder she was upset. 'It proved to me,' she writes, 'that

ANTHONY TROLLOPE, Julia Margaret Cameron, 1864

detail of table cover, chair and crinoline skirt were essential to the judges of the art.'

Her greatest portraits, such as the 1867 picture of Thomas Carlyle (1795–1881), show her determined resistance to the virtues of *Brenda*. Carlyle was the most celebrated literary man in London, the 'sage of Chelsea' – a gruff, grumbling historian and satirist who could tell the modern world what was wrong with it, although unfortunately had no prescription for setting it right. Handsome and intense, he was painted, sculpted and photographed to an enormous degree – David Piper's *The English Face* devotes a whole chapter to his many portraits (overlooking the fact that Carlyle's face was Scottish).

Of the two extant photographs of Carlyle by Mrs Cameron, this profile of Carlyle as Old Testament prophet is perhaps less well known than the one captioned 'Carlyle like a rough block of Michael Angelo's sculpture', but it is a stupendously luminous picture, nevertheless, almost a hologram. Carlyle considered portraiture an essential aid to history, and was a trustee of the National Portrait Gallery. 'Often have I found a portrait superior in real instruction to half a dozen biographies,' he wrote, 'or, rather let me say, I have found the portrait was a small lighted candle by which the biographies could for the first time be read.' By such an analogy, this photograph by Mrs Cameron is a veritable lantern.

Her 1864 portrait of the prolific and popular Anthony Trollope (1815–82) is another prophet picture, rendered rather less high-flown by the unusual and emphatic presence of his hat. Trollope was not a High Art sort of writer, and at this time he still held his job at the Post Office, where he was responsible for introducing the pillar box into England. From the same sitting

CHARLES DARWIN, Julia Margaret Cameron, 1868

to Mrs Cameron, taken while Trollope was holidaying at Freshwater, there is another portrait, without the hat, which reveals the usual huge 'seat of intellect'. But the picture reproduced here depicts the man much more strongly than the other. The symmetry of the picture, with its natural square framing of Trollope's clever face, conveys more humanity and wit.

Although it is easy to think of Mrs Cameron as an amateur photographer, pottering at home with gallons of water and wet collodion plates, she was not by any means a smatterer. Her hundreds of images were marketed, and printed, by the Colnaghi Gallery, although her insistence on top-quality paper and printing often meant profits were eroded. Sometimes the prints were sold with inscriptions; and this 1868 picture of Charles Darwin (1809–82) was inscribed on several copies by Darwin himself.

'I like this photograph very much better than any other which has been taken of me,' he wrote, over and over. Only Mrs Cameron, one feels, could persuade the greatest scientist of the age to sit down and sign pictures for her, so that she could sell them. And what a long, unnecessary sentence he misguidedly chose, when he might equally have written 'Excellent! (Charles Darwin)' in a fraction of the time.

GEORGE FREDERIC WATTS (1817–1904)

'What I try for is the half-conscious insistence upon the nobilities of the subject,' G. F. Watts said of portrait painting – which perhaps only goes to confirm that 'half-conscious' had a rather different meaning a hundred years ago. The splendour of his self-portrait of *c.*1879, very

GEORGE FREDERIC WATTS, self-portrait, *c.*1879

consciously modelled on Titian, has clearly not achieved nobility through accident. Although his widow, compiling her catalogue of Watts's portraits, disliked his 'strenuous' expression in many of his self-portraits, she surely would not have argued with the emphatic beauty of this picture. In life, apparently, Watts was modest, sensitive to his own failings, and although highly productive, the least strenuous personality anyone ever met. But in this self-portrait, this deliberate gift to posterity, either he could not disguise his true self-worth, or simply did not know how to paint someone who was not a latter-day Venetian genius. Either way, the result is one of his finest portraits – warm, sonorous and deeply attractive.

Just as Mrs Cameron's lack of personal beauty gave her an obsession with it (her last word, as she lay dying in Ceylon, was 'Beautiful'), so perhaps Watts's disadvantaged background explains his slightly undignified, almost naïve slavishness to the Victorian greats. His father was a piano tuner, and he received no formal education, inherited no money. Yet by talent alone, he rose to the comfortable position of 'Il Signor' at Little Holland House, where according to George du Maurier he was served tea by women 'almost kneeling' and 'worshipped till his manliness had almost departed'. It was a strange life, by modern standards. Lapdog, honoured guest, what was he? Very little was evidently required of Watts in return for his residency. Once asked by a patron to teach children to draw, he is supposed to have responded by putting a brick on the table with the words 'Draw that.' Although educationally sound, this peevish response promptly put an end to such requests.

Watts was an extremely productive painter who nevertheless is always described in a state of benign calm, or delicate headache, or forlorn exhaustion; his output and his reported character are hard to reconcile. His projects were not the projects of a lazy or a sickly man – massive murals on grand historical themes, symbolic tableaux on cosmic truths, the 'Hall of Fame' portraits painted with an eye firmly fixed on the future gratitude of posterity. One begins to suspect that he lay moaning on sofas with hand pressed lightly against brow only until the room was cleared, at which point he leapt up, locked the door, and impersonated a tornado. On his death, he left eight hundred canvases, which hardly squares with Lord Holland's early description of him as 'terribly dilatory and indolent . . . I fear he has not the energy and qualities to ensure his prosperity in the world.'

Patronage suited Watts well; apart from the financial security, it made him feel more Italian. His first patrons, Lord and Lady Holland, he met in Italy in 1843; on his return to England in 1847 he fell in with the famous Pattles, from whose influence he did not emerge for twenty-five years. (Under *his* influence, incidentally, they eschewed the fashion for crinoline skirts, and chose full, heavy dresses that fell into the romantic folds he loved to paint.) Marriage might have galvanised him to a more independent life, but unfortunately, when his friends persuaded him to marry the teenage Ellen Terry

GEORGE FREDERIC WATTS, Henry Herschel Hay Cameron, n.d.

in 1864, the result was predictably a disaster, and the couple were separated within the year.

The problem was obvious. Ellen Terry was young and headstrong, very much the heroine of her own life, and Watts soon found that he disapproved of her. 'It was the misfortune of Watts always to be moving in a circle "above his station"', observed his biographer Wilfrid Blunt, on this marriage question. 'He never came across piano tuners' daughters.' Although the Pattles were bohemians, they were well-born; they clearly thought a pretty little actress would be good enough for their 'Signor'. The more one examines the marriage of Watts to Ellen Terry, in fact, the more unforgivable looks the presumption of the artist's 'friends'.

His second marriage, to Mary Fraser-Tytler in 1886, was a far less tempestuous affair. The only similarity was that, at nearly seventy, he was the same age as Mary's father, just as he had been the same age as Ellen's in 1864. Mary was devoted to Signor, and her belief in his genius can be quite refreshing when to modern eyes his grand, symbolic work appears unfashionably high flown. In her three-volume biography of Watts, *Annals of an Artist's Life* (1912), she wrote a touching and pictorial description of a meeting at Freshwater – watching with a friend as Watts, Tennyson and his son Hallam come into view:

> For down the great aisle of elms they came, a white Russian deer-hound
> flashing like silver through the sun or shade, and the central figure the poet,
> a note of black in the midst of the vivid green, grand in the folds of his
> ample cloak and his face looming grandly from the shadow of the giant hat
> . . . And then our eye fell upon the delicate grey figure of our beloved painter
> on the other side, the grey hat crowning silver hair, a grey cloak taking
> pleasant folds while he stepped like a boy, light and neat in every movement.

His admirers called him 'the Divine Watts'; they perceived in him humility and a child-like quality, which made them want to support him. One must suppose all this kitten-in-basket helplessness was genuine, however much the characters of Dickens interfere with all our perceptions of Victorian gentlefolk who profess themselves mere children about money. 'There was something pathetic to me in the occasional poise of the head,' wrote a Miss Ellice Hopkins on meeting Watts on the Isle of Wight. 'The face slightly lifted, as we see in the blind, as if in dumb beseeching to the fountain of Eternal Beauty for more power to think his thoughts for him.'

Few artists had a firmer pact with posterity than Watts, which makes it the sadder that his mistakes and aspirations have survived to mock him. But his triumphs are triumphs still; his grandiose and sombre 'Hall of Fame' paintings are invaluable for their concision and sensitivity; and his portrait of Ellen Terry – *Choosing* (page 41) – is a successful symbolic painting as well as a portrait. Likewise his beautiful *Tennyson* of *c*.1863–4 (page 4), backed with bayleaves, a strip of coastline and a deep blue night sky, is a masterpiece.

THE MUCH PHOTOGRAPHED HOUSEHOLD
AT DIMBOLA

It is an odd thing that both Watts and Mrs Cameron are sometimes accused of Pre-Raphaelitism. There are worse things, of course. But custodians of their work tend to grow impatient with the PRB label, and a plaintive 'Watts NOT a Pre Raphaelite' used to be the hand-written sign pinned to the Gothic door of the Watts Gallery at Compton in Surrey, signed by Watts's curator and biographer Wilfrid Blunt. The confusion arises, perhaps, from the PRB's liking for the same sort of subjects – biblical, a bit of Camelot and Shakespeare, Gothic gates, men with beards, glum long-faced girls with their hair unpinned. While other Victorian artists might paint railway scenes and race meetings, both the PRB and the Watts-Cameron coalition (or WCC) were artistically attracted more to the walled monastic garden, or the scene of perfect calm.

But the aims of the WCC were quite different from those of the PRB. In terms of style and technique G. F. Watts aspired to Renaissance art; he preached sublimity, ideality and emotional expression. Mrs Cameron's husband Charles Hay Cameron wrote a treatise on the sublime, in which he stressed qualities of 'unconquerable fortitude' and 'tender remembrance'. So the rather bizarre result was that while the Pre-Raphaelites were busy copying the clarity of photography, Mrs Cameron was using photography to pursue the poetry of art. This was brave and stubborn of her; it meant denying the plain truth that photography is not really capable of producing an 'ideal' image, however energetically you wish the case were otherwise.

Her tableaux and allegorical pictures are, in a way, anti-portraits. They are pictures, or idylls, using real-life models whose actual identity is deemed unimportant by the artist. *Rebecca*, the title of the picture might be, when discovered in the National Portrait Gallery's archive – and in brackets, underneath, 'Mrs Donkin's Cook'. Historians interested in the typology of Mrs Cameron's pictures grow impatient with this pin-the-name-on-the-sitter approach, and they are right, in a way. If Mrs Cameron called her *Rebecca*, that is what we should see. Yet there are some of us who just cannot help enjoying the idea of Mrs Donkin's cook (or even Mrs Donkin) being dragged out of historical obscurity, dressed up in a heavy

The Angel at the Sepulchre
(Mary Ann Hillier), Julia
Margaret Cameron, 1869

necklace and beaded head-
scarf, and posing immo-
bile for five minutes in
Mrs Cameron's converted
chicken-shed (her studio).

The almost random
bestowal of immortality was
the immediate effect of
photography, even when
as elevated in its aims as
this. Mrs Cameron's maid
Mary Hillier, hired at Freshwater, never wrote an epic
poem or rolled up her
sleeves for the Risorgi-
mento, but because of Mrs
Cameron's pictures, her face
is as well known as Tennyson's or Garibaldi's. With her female subjects,
Mrs Cameron is notably less interested in displaying the gigantic intellectual brow, and Mary Hillier's strengths were her cheeks, eyes and (in
particular) lips, features that she could compose into an expression of total,
beautiful, all-purpose vacancy. 'Goodness', 'Love', 'St Agnes', 'La Beata'
and countless Madonnas – all were embodied by Mary Hillier. As the
sublime *Angel at the Sepulchre*, she might equally be Mary Magdalene, a role
she frequently played. After all, technically the angel at the sepulchre
was male – but I doubt Mary Hillier ever engaged Mrs Cameron for long in
rigorous scriptural debate.

The Angel at the Sepulchre contrasts well with the bizarre group (is it in
fact a collage?) featuring Mrs Cameron's other 'Mary' – her semi-adopted
daughter Mary Ryan. While the *Angel* resembles a Bible illustration, *May
Day* is more like a caption competition. 'Who are these people, and what

36

May Day (Mary Ryan, Mary Ann Hillier, Freddy Gould and Kate Keown), Julia Margaret Cameron, 1866

on earth are they doing?' The child is dressed for a South Seas adventure, while the girl on the right has stepped from a picture by John Everett Millais. Sinister foliage abounds. The girl in the middle has an enormous face, which looms. And the various crazy sight-lines are so unsettling that if you look at it for long, you start to find yourself glancing worriedly over your shoulder.

In such a case, it is essential to know who the people are. For example, the boy is Freddy Gould, the child of a Freshwater labourer and sailor, who sacrificed his entire infancy to baring his little chest for Mrs Cameron's art. He was a perfect infant for all occasions, broad of brow and with terrific hair. Meanwhile Mary Hillier plays a rare subordinate role in the top left, and Kate Keown (daughter of a master gunner at Freshwater Redoubt, whose younger siblings often wore wings for Mrs Cameron) looks earnest below her. The overdressed girl is not identified, but I really do like her hat.

In splendour, in the middle, is Mary Ryan, an Irish girl originally found by Mrs Cameron begging with her mother on Putney Heath. This is one of her few starring parts, and she is making the most of it, bizarre though it is. Hers was an oddly unclassifiable life. Half-maid, half-daughter, she was educated with the Cameron boys but then dressed up in a plain white apron to draw water from the well. Far better educated than Mary Hillier, she made a superior marriage, but in the context of

King Ahasuerus and Queen Esther (Henry Taylor, Mary Ryan, Mary Kellaway), Julia Margaret Cameron, 1865

the Cameron photographs, she is emphatically the Cinderella of the story. Mary Hillier took all the plum roles, because of her endlessly interpretable blank expression, whereas Mary Ryan's efforts somehow never succeeded in disguising the fact that she is a maid dressed up in a smock.

Mary Ryan's acting abilities are plainly stretched to the limit in the tableau entitled *King Ahasuerus and Queen Esther*, based on a story from the Apocrypha. This was quite a popular image in its day, perhaps because it features the poet Henry Taylor holding a poker. Mrs Cameron described Taylor as a poet superior even to Tennyson (Tennyson responded that Taylor had a 'smile like a fish'), and was very grateful to him for assisting her efforts. He not only played a depressed Ahasuerus; he played a depressed King David in the same costume. Looking at these pictures, one sometimes feels like a spy watching someone's amateur theatricals; moreover theatricals that have gone awry. Noticeably, Tennyson never posed as anybody historical or fictional. In retrospect, this seems the act of a very sagacious man.

But Mrs Cameron photographed him anyway – by photographing the pictures he wrote. Her *Queen Rose of the Rosebud Garden of Girls* is a quotation from *Maud; The Gardener's Daughter* (a long shot outdoors of Mary Ryan) relates to his poem of the same name. Meanwhile his *Idylls of the King* became a life-culminating project for Mrs Cameron, who illustrated two volumes of the great Arthurian poems with large plates, and published them in 1875. It was an enterprise from which she hoped to make serious money, but although many of the pictures are beautiful, it did her little good in any respect. It was these *Idylls* that made George Bernard Shaw conclude, 'There is a terrible truthfulness about photography that sometimes makes a thing ridiculous.'

Mrs Cameron expended all her usual crash-bang efforts in search of models. A porter from Yarmouth was chosen as King Arthur; her husband Charles (praised by a reviewer for his surrender of 'every mental faculty') was Merlin; Agnes Mangles, a family friend, was Vivien; a role she modelled for in several photographs. As always, Mrs Cameron combined her models regardless of social rank, and regardless, too, of what they thought of it. 'I have been lying on the floor for the past two hours clutching the porter's ankle,' reported the model for *Guinevere*. It was a casual visit to Mrs Cameron that she would probably never forget.

Vivien and Merlin (Agnes Mangles and Charles Hay Cameron), Julia Margaret Cameron, 1874

ELLEN TERRY (1847–1928)

The reasons given for the unlikely marriage between Ellen Terry and G. F. Watts in February 1864 rarely strike a convincing note. Ellen was nearly seventeen at the time – although she always knocked a year off her age, and said she was nearly sixteen. But either way, Watts was thirty years older, with a bald patch and a bushy beard, the perfect embodiment of premature December, while she was glamorous and theatrical, and May all over. Did they fall in love? Were they pushed into matrimony by Julia Margaret Cameron's interfering sister Sara Prinsep, who thought it would do him good? Or did Watts just admire Ellen's lifelong ability to arrange herself in pleasing shapes, and want to rescue her from the stage? What is clear is that at Little Holland House, where Ellen and her sister Kate were invited in 1863 to pose for Watts, the painter found her deeply attractive, while she enthusiastically worshipped the beauty of his pictures. So if there is one thing we do know about this marriage, it is that it was founded on Art – even if Ellen later confessed to George Bernard Shaw that she felt naïvely obliged to marry Watts once he had kissed her passionately: 'I *must* be married to him *now*,' she wrote, 'because I was going to have a baby !!!'

'*Choosing*' is a symbolic picture, in which Watts quite beautifully represents the choice between the showy, scentless camellias that surround Ellen, and the humble violets she holds unnoticed in her raised left hand. Wearing the satin dress designed for her wedding by Holman Hunt, Ellen is outstandingly radiant – the embodiment of the verse in Tennyson's *Maud* about 'Queen rose of the rosebud garden of girls' – except that the flowers are not roses. At first glance, this picture is about Ellen's own moral choice between the life of the stage (blowsy hothouse blooms) and life married to Watts (modest but fresh and genuine, and a bit obscure). But the more one observes it, the more it seems obvious that Ellen is a bloom herself, as yet unpicked, and that the picture's power comes from the temptation of the painter, who is almost (but not quite) overcome by the yearnings of love.

Ellen did not possess classic beauty. Charles Reade, a writer whom she counted as her dearest friend, wrote in a notebook,

Ellen Terry is an enigma. Her eyes are pale, her nose rather long, her mouth nothing in particular. Complexion a delicate brickdust, her hair rather like

ELLEN TERRY (*'Choosing'*), George Frederic Watts, *c.*1864

tow. Yet somehow she is beautiful. Her expression kills any pretty face you see beside it.

What she clearly had, however, was a tremendous ability to create pictures on stage, and to make audiences (and possibly Watts) fall in love with her. She had already been on the stage eight years when she married Watts, having first appeared as the infant Mamilius in *The Winter's Tale* for Charles Kean in 1856. She was always a promising star, if at first overshadowed by her sister Kate, and she presumably already knew well her powers of attraction by the age of seventeen, even if she knew pitifully little about sex. Her son Edward Gordon Craig later described her as 'unmarriable' – and one guesses from this that perhaps she devoted so much energy to feminine allure that she did not have a lot left over for day-to-day married life. But when Watts pronounced the marriage experiment over, at the end of 1864, she was broken-hearted to return home. 'Incompatibility of temper' was the formal reason for the separation, which Ellen later confessed frankly '*more* than covered the ground'. But she was not at all happy about it. 'I was miserable, indignant, unable to understand that there could be any justice in what had happened.'

Had Watts supposed he was marrying a picture, a dream of beauty? After the separation, he is said to have destroyed many of his pictures of Ellen; *Choosing* escaped because it was already promised to a buyer. But Ellen continued to make pictures without him, by returning to the theatre. 'Her charm held everyone,' wrote her friend Graham Robertson, later, 'but I think preeminently those who loved pictures. She was *par excellence* the Painter's Actress and appealed to the eye before the ear; her gesture and pose were eloquence itself.' Reviews of Ellen's performances frequently mention artists' names – Veronese, Burne-Jones, Rossetti. Ellen was always personally charming ('Part of her remarkable mental endowment was a sure touch with men,' said Shaw). But it was her 'picturesque-ness' that everyone remarked on. Henry James wrote for the New York *Nation* of 1879:

She is greatly the fashion at present, and she belongs properly to a period which takes a strong interest in aesthetic furniture, archaeological attire, and blue china. Miss Ellen Terry is 'aesthetic'; not only her garments but her features themselves bear a stamp of the new enthusiasm.

Her career was interrupted twice. First, by her marriage to Watts, and then by her liaison with theatrical designer Edward Godwin, by whom she had two illegitimate children. Respectable people, such as her own parents, disowned her during this second romantic phase, but she bounced back. Even a disastrous second marriage to a drunkard fellow-actor did not repress her. Her own character seems remarkably similar, in fact, to the description she once gave of *Othello*'s Desdemona – unconventional, fiercely faithful, strong-willed. 'She is not at all prim or demure,' she noted. 'On the contrary, she is genially expressive, the kind of woman who being devoid of coquetry behaves as she feels.'

Certainly, however much people disapproved of the 'unmarriable' Ellen Terry, her self-belief meant they could never get the better of her. As Portia in *The Merchant of Venice*, she rocked theatrical London in 1879, when she touched her lover Bassanio in the casket scene. 'Good heavens, she's touching him!' said someone sitting next to Henry James, who was equally appalled. John Ruskin wrote a letter of protest to her director and co-star Henry Irving, recommending that she back off from Bassanio at least 'half a dozen yards'.

ELLEN TERRY, Herbert Barraud, n.d.

How much of this splendid personality is discernible in her portraits is an interesting question. Ellen has great presence in all of them – even when posed to compete with the wallpaper, as in Barraud's photograph. A niggling

ELLEN TERRY, George Frederic Watts, *c.*1864–5

question of attribution hangs over the 1864 Julia Margaret Cameron portrait (the wallpapered background is characteristic of Oscar Rejlander's work), but nevertheless it shows Ellen's perfect understanding of the part she played in her marriage to Watts – virginally alluring, soft and warm against a cool plain wall, reflective, isolated, her face in shadow. Her hair has been arranged to give a better view of her neck. It seems unlikely that Mrs Cameron sanctioned the expanse of bare flesh, or the sensuous back lighting, yet it is easy to imagine her admiring the picture for the poise and grace many people have admired in it since.

Famously, the larger part of Ellen's stage career (nearly twenty-five years) was spent with Henry Irving at the Lyceum Theatre. Irving was a show-

Sadness (Ellen Terry), Julia Margaret Cameron, 1864

man, and he chose Ellen well. At a time when theatre was enjoying an aesthetic heyday, Irving strove to create pictures by gaslight, and Ellen helped him. Their twenty-seven productions together were legendary, and even if Shaw was continually rude about him ('He does not merely cut plays, he disembowels them,' Shaw reported in 1896 in *Saturday Review*), Irving's grand, energetic manner of acting was popular and successful. Ellen's own great strengths, we are told, were her vivacity and expressiveness, and her command of pathos, and Irving adored her. When he finally got the chance to watch her from the stalls, he reported 'I wish I could tell you of the dream of beauty that you realised.' But then, people were always saying things like that to Ellen Terry.

ELLEN TERRY AS LADY
MACBETH, John
Singer Sargent,
1889

If any proof of Ellen's mature stardom were needed, John Singer Sargent's *Ellen Terry as Lady Macbeth* will do perfectly. 'Actors are the only artists who never see the work we are producing,' Ellen once complained, 'I would give ten years of my life to see myself act, that I might learn what to avoid.' But when she saw this picture, she must surely have been grateful for the big clue it contained. For this *Macbeth* production in 1888, her costume designer Alice Comyns-Carr spared no expense. The fine yarn for the dress was bought in Bohemia, the cloak of shot velvet was embroidered with griffins in flame-coloured tinsel, and green beetle wings were sewn on, to add metallic lustre, or feminine armour. The critics did not much like the show, but they went away dazzled by that costume, which is preserved at Ellen Terry's house at Smallhythe in Kent. Oscar Wilde wrote of the production: 'Judging from the banquet, Lady Macbeth seems an economical housekeeper, and evidently patronizes local industries for her husband's clothes and the servants' liveries; but she takes care to do all her own shopping in Byzantium.'

Technically, Ellen Terry is peripheral to Tennyson's circle. She spent just ten months in it, in 1864, was nearly crushed by it, and then made an extraordinary life elsewhere. She was fond of the laureate, however; she later starred in Tennyson's plays at the Lyceum, and she remembered forever that he had taught her to say 'luncheon' instead of 'lunch'. But she belongs here, surely, as the muse of everybody. While Tennyson, Watts, Mrs Cameron and Charles Dodgson were all hard at work worshipping beauty, Ellen Terry just had it, and moreover knew very well how to use it. Even if it meant artists and critics were continually defining her in their own terms, her projected beauty was born of a conscious decision to make her own life picturesque.

'Ellen Terry is the most beautiful name in the world,' wrote George Bernard Shaw. 'It rings like a chime through the last quarter of the nineteenth century.' He was infatuated, admittedly. But he certainly was not alone.

HENRY TAYLOR (1800–86)

When Henry Taylor stopped shaving in 1859, he had no idea of the repercussions for the history of photography. Having suffered increasingly with asthma attacks, he just decided (rather sensibly) not to hold an open razor to his throat any more. But then along came Julia Margaret Cameron, who idolised his poetry and worshipped facial hair, and the result was that he became the most photographed of all her male friends, his resplendent wiry beard and patent good nature making him the model sitter that Tennyson always refused to be.

Taylor's poetry is unread today, but when his Elizabethan-style verse drama *Philip van Artevelde* was published in 1834, it set him in the first rank of poetry. In fact, when Tennyson was made laureate in 1850, he beat Henry Taylor to the post. But Taylor had a proper job at the Colonial Office, writing policy documents on such important matters as slavery, so his 'Life Poetic' took second place until he finally retired at seventy-two. His collection of essays *The Statesman* (1836) unfortunately missed its mark; it was meant as gentle irony (on succeeding in politics by forgetting your friends, et cetera), but was tragically mistaken for serious advice.

Nowadays he is best known for his autobiography of 1885, which shows a pleasant, and surprisingly modern, preference for self-deprecation:

> *I was photographed, I think, almost every day, and the photographs being sent to Alice* [his wife], *her opinion was more flattering to them than to me: '. . . Most of them I think very grand: decidedly grander than anything you have yet written or lived; so I expect to think great things of you'.*

Taylor turned down promotion, and also refused the government of Upper Canada, which suggests he was very much his own man. He was not taken in by the flattery of Sara Prinsep's Little Holland House, either, which likewise indicates a remarkably steadfast nature. So, despite all Mrs Cameron's attempts to shower him with gifts, his fondness for her remained genuine, and he sympathised with Mr Cameron, whom he envisaged waking up one day to find no stick of worldly goods not given away. Clearly he enjoyed his friends immensely, and visited Freshwater twice a year. Dimbola, he said, reminded him of the old English squire who said 'This is Liberty Hall, and if everybody doesn't do as he likes here, by God, I'll make him!'

HENRY TAYLOR, Julia Margaret Cameron, c.1866

EDWARD LEAR (1812–88)

❧

'Come and meet Lear,' Tennyson used to say to people, 'not the king but the artist.' He was evidently so proud of this joke that he would often repeat it. Poor Edward Lear, having to put up with that sort of thing. Here he was, a shy, brilliant landscape artist, devoted to Emily Tennyson, happy to set Tennyson's poems to music, afflicted with the very same epilepsy, depression and poverty Alfred always feared for himself, and Tennyson kept making this terrible joke at his expense. No wonder he went abroad finally, and never came back.

Edward Lear was such a loner and wanderer that to include him in anybody's 'circle' is obviously stretching things. But his case is interesting here, partly because he was living proof that possession of talent and a beard was not everything. Mrs Cameron did not photograph him; Watts did not paint him. Although a frequent visitor to Farringford, he was clearly considered neither successful nor handsome enough for either honour. As an artist, he was not at all interested in portraiture, either; his landscapes were generally figureless. His career started with zoological painting – his 1832 *The Family of Psittacidae* (on parrots) was one of the first volumes of coloured plates on birds to be published in England, and it is a riot of tropical colour and wry characterisation. It did not make his fortune, alas. Later, he turned to travel and watercolour. Ironically, the one talent he did not rely on for money was nonsense verse.

If Lear did not conform to the aesthetics of 'Pattledom', neither did he like the Pattles very much. In fact he positively disliked Mrs Cameron with her 'odious incense palaver and fuss'.

EDWARD LEAR, self-portrait, 1864

He was a shy but quite opinionated man, and an astute observer, who 'wept like beans' when Tennyson read to him, but still disliked the way Alfred took Emily for granted. 'How I like him,' said the infant Lionel Tennyson once, when Lear left. Although the visits were never a complete success, his regret at leaving made him sad. He wrote to Emily, 'Such rare flashes of light make the path darker after they are over.'

His self-portrait from a letter of 1864 is one of several self-carica-tures. In its mixture of humour, sadness and yearning it is typical of the man, and might be seen as the visual equivalent of his self-portrait in his poem 'The Yonghy-Bonghy-Bo':

EDWARD LEAR, McLean, Melhuish & Haes, *c*.1862

> *'I am tired of living singly, –*
> *On this coast so wild and shingly, –*
> *I'm a-weary of my life:*
> *If you'll come and be my wife,*
> *Quite serene would be my life!' –*
> *Said the Yonghy-Bonghy-Bo,*
> *Said the Yonghy-Bonghy-Bo.*

Meanwhile, the *carte-de-visite* from *c*.1862 confirms Frank Lushing-ton's description of his friend, 'A face partly of Socrates, partly of Sir John Falstaff'. Photographically, however, it is typically functional.

'PATTLEDOM': THE PATTLE FAMILY

Opinion is divided as to who invented the collective noun 'Pattle-dom' for the forceful sisters of Julia Margaret Cameron. Some say it was William Makepeace Thackeray; Virginia Woolf says it was Sir Henry Taylor. All that is beyond doubt is its aptness, for the Pattles were a world unto themselves – and when people were singled out to be Pattled, *they knew they had been Pattled*. Before leaving India, Mrs Cameron had been the principal European hostess in Calcutta, and the position had bred imperiousness. She and her sisters were undeniable. They expected to organise London society as they had organised Calcutta's. In fact, trailing delicate incense and sandalwood in their wake, these feminine women call vividly to mind that other great invention of the Indian sub-continent, the all-crushing juggernaut.

HENRY THOBY PRINSEP, Julia Margaret Cameron, 1864

The seven Pattle sisters were born in India to an English father, James Pattle, and a French mother, Adeline, of aristocratic descent. James Pattle was evidently a hard-drinking man and a far-fetched romancer, over whom there hangs a fair amount of mystery. When Edward Lear later travelled in India, he was pleased to hear rumours of Pattle as a ludicrously boastful man, nicknamed 'Joot Singh, the King of Liars'. But as we have seen, Lear was no friend of Mrs Cameron, and it is possible the true King of Liars was some other chap altogether. What is better documented (though still not totally reliable) is the story that when James Pattle died in 1845, his body was shipped home to England for burial in a cask of spirits, which exploded on voyage, ejecting his body like a jack-in-the-box. The shock of this gruesome event is supposed to have killed his widow (who certainly died on the ship).

By the time the Pattles made their impact in London – in the 1850s and 1860s – most were married to men of distinction. Julia's elderly husband Charles Hay Cameron was not just a Benthamite philosopher and aesthete of the sublime, he was the son of the governor of the Bahamas, and had retired from a distinguished colonial career in Indian law and education.

JOHN JACKSON, Julia Margaret Cameron, n.d.

Meanwhile Sara Pattle had married the genial, high-ranking Indian civil servant Thoby Prinsep. The beautiful Virginia's husband was Lord Eastnor (3rd Earl Somers); Sophia's was John Dalrymple of the East India Company; Maria (known as Mia) married Dr John Jackson, one of Calcutta's leading physicians (she was the most intellectual of the sisters). And finally Louisa Pattle was married to Henry Vincent Bayley, who rose to be Judge of the Supreme Court of Calcutta. (The eldest sister, Adeline, the wife of a Scottish army officer, had died in 1836.)

Julia Margaret Cameron did not often photograph her sisters, but her portraits of their children and husbands are among her finest works. Her two brothers-in-law Thoby Prinsep (1792–1878) and John Jackson (1804–87) are superbly vivid in her portraits of them. Just as she photographed her own husband with his 'beard dipped in moonlight', so she pictured her sisters' husbands as benign versions of God. Prinsep was a

53

large man with a commanding presence; in India, when he opposed the future Lord Macaulay on educational issues, the two men were described as 'butting one another like bulls'. On retirement in London, however, he revealed a gentler side to his nature, as a generous host at Little Holland House, and a supporter of his wife's enthusiasm for artists and writers. Watts said his company was 'like turning the pages of a delightful book . . . open if you wanted it and shut when you did not'. Just a few days before his death, he discovered a new method of proving the forty-seventh proposition of the first book of Euclid.

Meanwhile Julia Jackson (1846–95) was one of her aunt's favourite models. 'My favourite Picture, My Niece Julia' is the affectionate caption on one picture from 1867, taken just before her marriage to Herbert Duckworth. Julia appears under many names in histories of portrait photography, which would be confusing, were her face not so utterly distinctive. But the reason is simple: she married twice. Duckworth died in 1870, of an undiagnosed abscess which burst as he reached to pick a fig, and Julia was left a widow with two children (and pregnant with the third). This stupendous picture was taken in 1872, during the period of her widowhood, and surely inspired Mrs Cameron's verse 'On a Portrait' of 1875, which includes the lines:

> Here we have eyes so full of fervent love
> That but for lids behind which sorrow's touch
> Does press and linger, one could almost prove
> That Earth had loved her favourite overmuch.
>
> A mouth where silence seems to gather strength
> From lips so gently closed, that almost say,
> 'Ask not my story lest you hear at length
> Of sorrows where sweet hope has lost its way.'
>
> And yet the head is borne so proudly high,
> The soft round cheek, so splendid in its bloom,
> True courage rises thro' the brilliant eye,
> And great resolve comes flashing through the gloom.

If the words were written for another portrait, they certainly apply to Julia Duckworth in this picture. In 1878 Julia married the widower Leslie Stephen, and their children together included Vanessa (later Vanessa Bell) and Adeline Virginia (Virginia Woolf). Adeline was the much-loved Pattle name of Julia's French grandmother, but in Virginia's case it was silently dropped.

Charles Lutwidge Dodgson (Lewis Carroll)
(1832–98)

Charles Dodgson's relationship with Tennyson was a tenuous but interesting one, in that the friendship was all one way. An enthusiastic amateur photographer, Dodgson photographed Tennyson and his young sons at Coniston in 1857; he turned up uninvited at Farringford in 1859; and then appeared again unannounced in July 1864, to find Tennyson away on holiday. In a letter to his cousin William Wilcox, he referred to the 'inalienable right of a free-born Briton to make a morning call', which justified these visits. Evidently he was quite unaware of Tennyson's quite contrary feelings on the matter.

There were few things on which Dodgson and Tennyson were likely to see eye to eye. Tennyson hated parodies of his work; Dodgson was an excellent parodist. Tennyson disliked photography; Dodgson was a keen photographer. Tennyson was hopelessly dirty; Dodgson meticulously clean – and so on. In his diaries Dodgson never seems to worry about whether he was welcome or not at the homes of famous people, and his description of his visit to Farringford in 1859 (from a letter) paints such an interesting picture of Tennysonian hospitality that it is worth quoting at some length.

> There was a man painting the garden railings when I walked up to the house, of whom I asked if Mr. Tennyson were at home, fully expecting the answer 'No', so that it was an agreeable surprise when he said, 'He's there, sir,' and pointed him out, and, behold! he was not many yards off, mowing his lawn in a wide awake [hat] and spectacles. I had to introduce myself, as he is too short-sighted to recognise people, and when he had finished the mowing he was at, he took me into the house to see Mrs. Tennyson who, I was very sorry to find, had been ill . . . She was lying on a sofa, looking very worn and haggard, so that I stayed a very few minutes. She asked me to come to dinner that evening . . . but her husband revoked the invitation before I left, as he said he wished her to be as little excited as possible that evening, and begged I would drop in for tea that evening, and dine with them the next day.

Dodgson describes his subsequent tea and dinner as 'delightful', but to a dispassionate eye both occasions seem rather bumpy. At teatime,

Tennyson talked about his dreams, and made to Dodgson the now famous remark, 'You, I suppose, dream photographs?' When Dodgson spotted proof-sheets of 'The King's Idylls [sic]' on the laureate's desk, Tennyson refused to let him read them. Mrs Tennyson confessed herself too tired to look at Dodgson's photographs, which he had brought along specially in an album. On the following evening, when he raised a perfectly civil question, she sounds almost snappy:

> I asked Mrs Tennyson for an explanation of 'The Lady of Shalott', which has been so variously interpreted. She said that the original legend is in Italian, and that Tennyson only gave it as he found it, so that it is hardly fair to expect him to furnish an interpretation as well.

Dodgson was in his tender mid-twenties when these first encounters took place. He was not yet the author of the most famous children's book of all time. But though keenly aware of Tennyson's greatness – and the honour of meeting him – he was also aware of the respect due to himself as a gentleman, and of his various 'inalienable rights'. He was, in short, quite proud. The son of a clergyman, he had given a lot of thought to decorum. In fact it was on the twin rocks of his own punctiliousness and the Tennysons' rudeness that the relationship finally foundered in 1870. He wrote from Oxford to beg Tennyson's permission to read a pirated poem that had come into his possession; Emily wrote back

CHARLES LUTWIDGE DODGSON (Lewis Carroll), unknown photographer, 1852–60

CHARLES LUTWIDGE DODGSON (Lewis Carroll),
Hills & Saunders, n.d.

to say that a gentleman would not even ask. He wrote again, demanding an apology, and did not receive a reply. And so his friendship with the Tennysons was over.

For a man who made such an impact on the imagination of a century, Dodgson is a highly disappointing figure. There is no escaping the fact. The author of *Alice* should be an anarchic, expansive wit, yet we pore over his portraits looking for the merest inkling of humour, and all we get is a bachelor neatly buttoned and combed, like the eager oysters dressed up for their fateful walk in 'The Walrus and the Carpenter'. His career at Christ Church, as a mathematics don, was distinguished but unremarkable. Meanwhile his opinions were conventional, conservative, straightlaced. When his friend Mrs Watts (Ellen Terry) opted to live in sin with Edward Godwin, he dropped her. Only when she was respectable again (i.e. married to someone unsuitable) did he pick up the relationship, and try to understand the difficulties she faced as the abandoned wife of Watts.

What makes all biographies of Dodgson unsatisfying, therefore, is that he lived so much in his head. He spent sleepless hours entertaining himself – logical puzzles, anagrams, acrostic poems, parodies – and he was very creative at it. Yet his outward story – like his face – was a blank. Educated at Rugby and Oxford, he became a fellow of Christ Church and never left. He once took a trip to Russia. He had lots of jolly holidays in Eastbourne. He frequented the London theatre, as long as there was nothing indecent in the plays. The publication of his hugely successful books seems not to have changed his outlook on life in any way whatsoever.

One entry in his diary for 1865 recounts a typical day in London:

Nov: 30. (Th). *Went to the Winter Exhibition of British Artists and Mrs Cameron's Photographs. Called on Macmillan* [his publisher], *who tells me five hundred* Alices *are already sold. In the afternoon I went to see the Terrys. Got back to Christ Church about eight.*

He made visits all the time, and often took photographs of his illustrious friends, but the people he really liked (and who evidently liked him back) were pre-pubescent girls. So much is (unfortunately) famous about him, and it is a tragedy that sorting through this particular can of worms is virtually the principal responsibility of the modern Dodgson biographer, even though the question, Was he a pervert? can be confidently answered, No. Clearly Dodgson took an unusual interest in little girls – forever striking up friendships, in a manner that nowadays looks creepy. But it seems pretty clear, too, that he liked little girls because they were non-sexual. Moreover, entertaining little girls transported him back to his own childhood where, growing up in North Yorkshire in a household of girls, his earliest joy was to entertain his sisters with bits of nonsense verse and funny drawings.

In all his dealings with adults, Dodgson's character was like his portraits – self-conscious, prim, private. But with little girls he lost his stammer; he teased them and entertained them; he photographed them tenderly. If he also photographed them nude (on rare occasions), so did many other photographers at the time. Propriety was so much Dodgson's adult concern in all things, that when relations were mysteriously broken off between him and Alice Liddell (the Dean's daughter for whom *Alice's Adventures* were first written), it was surely not because he had proposed marriage to a twelve-year-old. More likely, he took umbrage at something himself. Like Tennyson, he was a touchy man. He also liked to keep his relationships under the strictest personal control.

Photography was a natural hobby for Dodgson. It was intimacy at a safe distance, and it also appealed to him in other ways. If Mrs Cameron wanted to 'arrest' the beauty that came before her, he wanted similarly to arrest childhood before it withered and waned. Critics have noted how unsettling it is in *Alice* that the heroine changes so many times, growing big and small, forgetting who she is. Dodgson had a very simple attachment to childhood. He yearned for it. In a poem called 'Solitude' he wrote:

> I'd give all wealth that years have piled,
>   The slow result of Life's decay,
> To be once more a little child
>   For one bright summer day.

And it was noticeable that Dodgson rarely retained a friendship with children once they started to mature. A rather chilling note in his 1865 diary records a sighting of Alice Liddell at the age of thirteen: 'Met Alice and Miss Prickett [the governess] in the quadrangle,' he says. 'Alice seems changed a good deal, and hardly for the better – probably going through the usual awkward stage of transition.'

As a fellow photographer, he did not approve of Mrs Cameron's pictures, but at least he knew what an effort it was to take photographs by the wet collodion process. His poem 'Hiawatha's Photographing' (see pages 62–3) was originally prefaced by a description of the whole smelly chemical business involved:

> First, a piece of glass he coated
> With collodion, and plunged it
> In a bath of lunar caustic
> Carefully dissolved in water –
> There he left it certain minutes.
>   Secondly, my Hiawatha
> Made with cunning hand a mixture
> Of the acid pyrro-gallic,
> And of glacial-acetic,
> And of alcohol and water –
> This developed all the picture.
>   Finally, he fixed each picture

With a saturate solution
Which was made of hyposulphite,
Which, again, was made of soda.
(Very difficult the name is
For a metre like the present
But periphrasis has done it.)

'Hiawatha's Photographing' is a marvellous, wicked description of Victorian portrait photography, but one cannot help feeling that the accommodating 'Hiawatha' in the poem is nothing much like the real Dodgson, whose pernickety perfectionism fairly demented his publishers and made enemies of his illustrators. If Dodgson did not like the quality of a print run, he would scrap it, send it to America, start again. If this meant the book was delayed for six months, so be it. Similarly, he bombarded his illustrators with instructions, hence Harry Furniss's good-natured picture of himself barring the door to Dodgson. When illustrating Dodgson's late books *Sylvie and Bruno* (1889) and *Sylvie and Bruno Concluded* (1893), he felt quite tormented by the author's requirements. Apart from anything else, 'How old is your model for Sylvie?' Dodgson would write to ask him, repeatedly; 'And may I have her name and address?'

<small>Charles Lutwidge Dodgson (Lewis Carroll) and Harry Furniss, Harry Furniss, before 1902</small>

'HIAWATHA'S PHOTOGRAPHING' BY LEWIS CARROLL
(FIRST PUBLISHED 1857, REVISED 1883)

From his shoulder Hiawatha
Took the camera of rosewood,
Made of sliding, folding rosewood;
Neatly put it all together.
In its case it lay compactly,
Folded into nearly nothing;
But he opened out the hinges,
Pushed and pulled the joints and hinges,
Till it looked all squares and oblongs,
Like a complicated figure
In the Second Book of Euclid.

This he perched upon a tripod –
Crouched beneath its dusky cover –
Stretched his hand, enforcing silence –
Said, 'Be motionless, I beg you!'
Mystic, awful was the process.

All the family in order
Sat before him for their pictures:
Each in turn as he was taken,
Volunteered his own suggestions,
His ingenious suggestions.

First the Governor, the Father:
He suggested velvet curtains
Looped about a massy pillar;
And the corner of a table,
Of a rosewood dining-table.
He would hold a scroll of something,
Hold it firmly in his left-hand;
He would keep his right-hand buried
(Like Napoleon) in his waistcoat;
He would contemplate the distance
With a look of pensive meaning,
As of ducks that die in tempests.

Grand, heroic was the notion:

Yet the picture failed entirely:
Failed, because he moved a little,
Moved, because he couldn't help it.

Next, his better half took courage;
She would have her picture taken.
She came dressed beyond description,
Dressed in jewels and in satin
Far too gorgeous for an empress.
Gracefully she sat down sideways,
With a simper scarcely human,
Holding in her hand a bouquet
Rather larger than a cabbage.
All the while that she was sitting,
Still the lady chattered, chattered,
Like a monkey in the forest.
'Am I sitting still?' she asked him.
'Is my face enough in profile?
Shall I hold the bouquet higher?
Will it come into the picture?'
And the picture failed completely.

Next the Son, the Stunning-Cantab:
He suggested curves of beauty,
Curves pervading all his figure,
Which the eye might follow onward,
Till they centred in the breast-pin,
Centred in the golden breast-pin.
He had learnt it all from Ruskin
(Author of 'The Stones of Venice',
'Seven Lamps of Architecture',
'Modern Painters', and some others);
And perhaps he had not fully
Understood his author's meaning;
But, whatever was the reason,
All was fruitless, as the picture

Ended in an utter failure.

   Next to him the eldest daughter:
She suggested very little,
Only asked if he would take her
With her look of 'passive beauty'.

   Her idea of passive beauty
Was a squinting of the left-eye,
Was a drooping of the right-eye,
Was a smile that went up sideways
To the corner of the nostrils.

   Hiawatha, when she asked him,
Took no notice of the question,
Looked as if he hadn't heard it;
But, when pointedly appealed to,
Smiled in his peculiar manner,
Coughed and said it 'didn't matter',
Bit his lip and changed the subject.

   Nor in this was he mistaken,
As the picture failed completely.

   So in turn the other sisters.

   Last the youngest son was taken:
Very rough and thick his hair was,
Very round and red his face was,
Very dusty was his jacket,
Very fidgety his manner.
And his overbearing sisters
Called him names he disapproved of:
Called him Johnny, 'Daddy's Darling',
Called him Jacky, 'Scrubby School-boy',
And, so awful was the picture,
In comparison the others
Seemed, to one's bewildered fancy,
To have partially succeeded.

   Finally my Hiawatha
Tumbled all the tribe together
('Grouped' is not the right expression),
And, as happy chance would have it

Did at last obtain a picture
Where the faces all succeeded:
Each came out a perfect likeness.

   Then they joined and all abused it,
Unrestrainedly abused it,
As the worst and ugliest picture
They could possibly have dreamed of.
'Giving one such strange expressions –
Sullen, stupid, pert expressions.
Really anyone would take us
(Anyone that did not know us)
For the most unpleasant people!'
(Hiawatha seemed to think so,
Seemed to think it not unlikely.)
All together rang their voices,
Angry, loud, discordant voices,
As of dogs that howl in concert,
As of cats that wail in chorus.

   But my Hiawatha's patience,
His politeness and his patience,
Unaccountably had vanished,
And he left that happy party.
Neither did he leave them slowly,
With the calm deliberation,
The intense deliberation
Of a photographic artist:
But he left them in a hurry,
Left them in a mighty hurry,
Stating that he would not stand it,
Stating in emphatic language
What he'd be before he'd stand it.
Hurriedly he packed his boxes:
Hurriedly the porter trundled
On a barrow all his boxes:
Hurriedly he took his ticket:
Hurriedly the train received him:
Thus departed Hiawatha.

LIST OF ILLUSTRATIONS

Alfred Tennyson, 1st Baron Tennyson, 1809–92
George Frederic Watts, c.1863–4
Oil on canvas, 61.3 x 51.4 cm
© National Portrait Gallery (1015)

Woolner at Farringford, 1857
Max Beerbohm, 1917
Watercolour, 33 x 26 cm
Tate Gallery, London 1999 (A01046)
© The Max Beerbohm Estate

Julia Margaret Cameron, 1815–79
Attributed to Lord Somers, n.d.
Albumen print, 15.3 x 11.3 cm (arched)
© National Portrait Gallery (x18000)

The Late Lord Tennyson: Mr G. F. Watts, RA, painting the Poet Laureate's Portrait in the Study at Farringford
Reginald Cleaver, 1892
Pen, 14 x 19.5 cm
© National Portrait Gallery (RN30483)

George Frederic Watts, 1817–1904 (with a cast for his sculpture *Physical Energy*)
Henry Herschel Hay Cameron, n.d.
Print from an original negative, 20.32 x 15.24 cm
© National Portrait Gallery (RN50447)

Alfred Tennyson, 1st Baron Tennyson, 1809–92
Attributed to James Spedding, c.1831
Pencil, 19.7 x 14 cm
© National Portrait Gallery (3940)

Alfred Tennyson, 1st Baron Tennyson, 1809–92
Samuel Laurence, c.1840
Oil on canvas, 67.9 x 57.8 cm
© National Portrait Gallery (2460)

Alfred Tennyson, 1st Baron Tennyson, 1809–92
Thomas Woolner, 1856
Plaster cast of medallion, 26 cm (diameter)
© National Portrait Gallery (3847)

Alfred Tennyson, 1st Baron Tennyson, 1809–92
Julia Margaret Cameron, 1869
Albumen print, 25.5 x 20 cm (arched top)
© National Portrait Gallery (x18023)

Emily Tennyson, 1813–96
W. Jeffrey, 1860s
Carte-de-visite photograph, 8.8 x 5.5 cm
© National Portrait Gallery (x12995)

Lionel Tennyson, 1854–86
Julia Margaret Cameron, 1864
Photograph, 25.8 x 19.3 cm
©NMPFT/Science & Society Picture Library

Julia Margaret Cameron, 1815–79
Henry Herschel Hay Cameron, 1870
Albumen print, 24.4 x 20.3 cm
© National Portrait Gallery (P696)

Thomas Carlyle, 1795–1881
Julia Margaret Cameron, 1867
Albumen print, printed in reverse, 33.7 x 28.6 cm
© National Portrait Gallery (P123)

Anthony Trollope, 1815–82
Julia Margaret Cameron, 1864
Albumen print, 25.4 x 19.7 cm
© National Portrait Gallery (P214)

Charles Darwin, 1809–82
Julia Margaret Cameron, 1868
Albumen print, 33 x 25.6 cm
© National Portrait Gallery (P8)

George Frederic Watts, 1817–1904
Self-portrait, c.1879
Oil on canvas, 63.5 x 50.8 cm
© National Portrait Gallery (1406)

George Frederic Watts, 1817–1904
Henry Herschel Hay Cameron, n.d.
Albumen print on card mount, 24 x 19 cm
© National Portrait Gallery (x20030)

The Angel at the Sepulchre (Mary Ann Hillier)
Julia Margaret Cameron, 1869
Albumen print, 37 x 26.7 cm
Royal Photographic Society Collection, Bath

May Day (Mary Ryan, Mary Ann Hillier, Freddy Gould and Kate Keown)
Julia Margaret Cameron, 1866
Albumen print on gold-edged cabinet mount, 11.5 x 9.6 cm
© National Portrait Gallery (x18039)

King Ahasuerus and Queen Esther (Henry Taylor, Mary Ryan, Mary Kellaway)
Julia Margaret Cameron, 1865
Photograph, 31.7 x 27.1 cm
©NMPFT/Science & Society Picture Library

Vivien and Merlin (Agnes Mangles and Charles Hay Cameron)
Julia Margaret Cameron, 1874
Albumen print, 32.2 x 25.6 cm
© National Portrait Gallery (x18029)

Ellen Terry ('*Choosing*'), 1847–1928
George Frederic Watts, c.1864
Oil on strawboard, 48 x 35.2 cm
© National Portrait Gallery (5048)

Ellen Terry, 1847–1928
Herbert Barraud, n.d.
Carbon print, 24.7 x 17.8 cm
© National Portrait Gallery (x26815)

Ellen Terry, 1847–1928
George Frederic Watts, c.1864–5
Oil on canvas, 59.7 x 59.7 cm
© National Portrait Gallery (2274)

Sadness (Ellen Terry)
Julia Margaret Cameron, 1864
Albumen print, 22.1 x 17.5 cm (oval)
The J.Paul Getty Museum, Los Angeles (84.XZ.186.52)

Ellen Terry, 1847–1928, as Lady Macbeth
John Singer Sargent, 1889
Oil on canvas, 2.21 x 1.14 m
© Tate Gallery, London 1999 (N02053)

Henry Taylor, 1800–86
Julia Margaret Cameron, c.1866
Albumen print, 24.2 x 19.9 cm
© National Portrait Gallery (x18020)

Edward Lear, 1812–88
Self-portrait, 1864
Pen and ink, 14 x 17.5 cm
© National Portrait Gallery (4351)

Edward Lear, 1812–88
McLean, Melhuish & Haes, c.1862
Albumen *carte-de-visite*, 9.2 x 5.7 cm
© National Portrait Gallery (AX17831)

Henry Thoby Prinsep, 1792–1878
Julia Margaret Cameron, 1864
Albumen print, 36.4 x 28.4 cm
© National Portrait Gallery (x18013)

John Jackson, 1804–87
Julia Margaret Cameron, n.d.
Albumen print, 31.5 x 25.8 cm (oval)
© National Portrait Gallery (x18009)

Mrs Herbert Duckworth (née Julia Jackson), 1846–95
Julia Margaret Cameron, 1872
Albumen print on gold-edged cabinet mount, 14.1 x 10.3 cm
© National Portrait Gallery (x18052)

Charles Lutwidge Dodgson (Lewis Carroll), 1832–98
Unknown photographer, 1852–60
Albumen print, 19.7 x 14.6 cm
© National Portrait Gallery (P39)

Charles Lutwidge Dodgson (Lewis Carroll), 1832–98
Hills & Saunders, n.d.
Sepia albumen print, 8.5 x 5.7 cm
© National Portrait Gallery (x5181)

Charles Lutwidge Dodgson (Lewis Carroll), 1832–98, and Harry Furniss, 1854–1925
Harry Furniss, before 1902
Pen and ink, 27.3 x 19.1 cm
© National Portrait Gallery (3567)